DEDICATION

This book is a dedication to my dad for allowing me
to take care of him as long as I could.

Love and miss you, Daddy.

Table of Contents

PREFACE:
STILL UNBROKEN: A WOMAN'S TRUTH ABOUT LOVE, RESPECT, AND CHOOSING HERSELF

There comes a time in every woman's life when she realizes she has more to say.

When the first book closes, but the lessons don't stop.

When the healing begins, but the truth still sits heavy on the heart.

Unbroken was the story of the little girl I once was. The one who survived abandonment, rejection, pain, abuse, heartbreak, and loss.

It was the story of where I came from, what I lived through, and how God carried me through storms I didn't think I would survive.

But this book right here...

This is the story of the woman I became after all of that.

When I wrote *Unbroken,* I thought I had emptied my soul.

I thought that book held everything, every hurt, every memory, every truth I had been carrying since childhood.

1

But time has a way of revealing the rest of the story.

Healing opens new doors.

And as I grew older, I realized there were things I never said, lessons I never shared, and wisdom that came only after the pain settled and life made me look at myself again.

This book is not about what broke me.

This book is about what I learned after the breaking.

It is about love, the real kind and the fake kind.

It is about respect, the foundation of everything.

It is about the lies people tell, the boundaries we must set, and the courage it takes to choose yourself even when your heart still wants to hold on.

It is about family, loyalty, gossip, disappointment, and the things you discover when people reveal their true colors.

It is about becoming a grown woman who is no longer afraid to speak the truth.

Unbroken showed the world who I was.

Still Unbroken shows the world who I am now.

Back then, I was sharing my story so that people could understand what had shaped me.

But now, I'm speaking to the women who lived through their own storms.

The women who gave too much.

The women who loved too hard.

The women who stayed too long.

The women who carried secrets, protected people who didn't protect them, and kept smiling when their hearts were tired.

This book is for every woman who has ever lost herself in someone else.

For every woman who thought she needed a man to complete her.

For every woman who waited for honesty and got excuses instead.

For every woman who had to pick herself up from a place she never should have been.

These pages are not written from the perspective of a broken girl.

They are written by a woman who survived everything meant to destroy her, and now walks with wisdom, clarity, and a strong sense of self-worth.

Still Unbroken is not a continuation of my pain. It is a continuation of my power.

It is me speaking my truth about relationships, respect, loyalty, boundaries, and the kind of love a woman deserves. It is me explaining why I refuse to settle, why I won't accept disrespect, and why today I choose myself, my peace, and the legacy I want to leave behind.

This book is shorter than my first one, but its truth is deeper.

Every chapter comes straight from the heart, no sugarcoating, no pretending, no hiding.

Just real talk from a woman who has lived, learned, and finally decided that choosing herself is not selfish... it is survival.

If *Unbroken* showed the world how I stood through the storm, then *Still Unbroken* shows the world how I walk forward, stronger, wiser, and still standing tall.

This is my truth.

This is my growth.

This is my next chapter.

And to every woman reading this, may you find your strength in these pages, and may you remember this one thing:

You may bend, you may hurt, you may cry... but you are still unbroken.

CHAPTER ONE:

THE WOMAN I BECAME AFTER THE HURT

There comes a moment in every woman's life when she sits quietly with herself and realizes she is no longer the person she used to be. Something shifts. The old wounds don't sting the same way. The old fears don't scare her the way they once did. And the pain that once swallowed her whole begins to feel like a story she lived through, not a story she is still living in.

I didn't understand that kind of moment when I was younger. Back then, I believed pain stayed forever. I believed the heartbreaks, the disappointments, the betrayals, and the losses would sit on my chest until my last breath. I believed the damage done to me made me unworthy of something better. When you grow up abandoned and confused, when your childhood is filled with questions nobody ever answers, you learn to hold your breath through storms. You learn to survive, not live.

My first book, *Unbroken*, was written from that place.

It was the voice of the little girl who kept picking herself up off the ground, again and again, trying to understand why life felt so heavy. It told the truth of where I came from, foster care, rejection, abuse, fear, loneliness, and loss. It told the truth of a girl who found love in her grandmother's arms and tried to rebuild a life from the pieces left behind.

But this book... this book is not about the girl I used to be.

This book is about the woman I am now.

- A woman who finally understands herself.

- A woman who lived long enough to see the patterns.

- A woman who no longer carries her wounds as shame but as wisdom.

- A woman who refuses to apologize for her truth.

This chapter starts where the first book ended, not with the pain, but with the awakening that came after.

Growing up, I imagined healing as some big, loud moment, like the sky opening up, the sun shining down, and God whispering in my ear, "Your heart is fixed now." But healing didn't come to me that way. It came slowly, quietly, sometimes painfully. It came in the form of realizations I didn't know I needed.

Healing came when I realized I had spent most of my life trying to prove I was worthy of love.

It came when I finally admitted to myself how deeply I wanted to be chosen, not as an option, not as a convenience, not as someone men entertained when they were lonely, but as a woman someone truly valued.

- It came when I started to see the difference between someone loving me and someone using the love I gave them.

- It came when I stopped blaming myself for the things other people did to me.

- It came when I looked in the mirror and saw a woman who had survived too much to settle for anything less than respect.

The woman I am today didn't appear overnight. She arrived after years of heartbreak that nearly broke me apart. She showed up after arguments that drained my spirit, after silence that felt like punishment, after apologies that were only meant to pull me back into cycles I had already outgrown. She came after I cried until my body felt empty. She came after I made mistakes, trusted the wrong people, held onto the wrong relationships, and ignored my own voice for the sake of keeping peace with others.

But the truth is, the peace I kept for other people always stole peace from myself.

One day, something in me just snapped. Not in anger, but in clarity. Something whispered, "You deserve better." And for the first time in my life, I actually believed it.

That was the beginning of the woman I became after the hurt.

- People see your strength long before you feel it.

- They see the way you keep getting back up.

- They see the way you continue loving people even after they've broken you.

- They see the way you forgive more than you should, fight for people who wouldn't fight for you, and carry weights that were never yours to carry.

But what they don't see is the moment you finally get tired.

I remember waking up one morning, not physically, but spiritually, and realizing I was exhausted from being strong. Not the kind of strong that makes you proud, but the kind of strong that makes you tired. The strong that comes from surviving instead of living. The strong that comes from protecting yourself instead of being protected.

From that moment on, something changed in me. I stopped letting people treat me like I was too easy to come back to. I stopped answering calls from people who only remembered I existed when they needed something. I stopped explaining myself to people who wanted to misunderstand me. I stopped shrinking to make other people comfortable. I stopped trying to fix relationships that were never meant to grow.

Instead, I started using my voice.

And that voice, the one I thought had been taken from me many times, became louder, stronger, clearer. Not loud in volume, but loud in truth.

People say, "You talk different now."

No!

I talk honest now.

People say, "You've changed."

No!

I've grown.

Growth scares people who don't want to grow with you.

As I stepped into this new version of myself, I started seeing life differently. I started paying attention to the small lessons hidden in everyday moments. I noticed how men speak to women. I noticed how women dim their light to keep relationships alive. I noticed how often love is confused with attachment. I noticed how many people pretend to care but listen only for information to gossip with. I noticed how people treat you according to how you treat yourself.

But the biggest thing I noticed was this:

Women forget their worth the moment they start believing someone else is responsible for their happiness.

- I was guilty of that.

- I gave too many chances.

- I confused effort with love.

- I accepted excuses I shouldn't have accepted.

- I allowed disrespect just because I didn't want to start over.

- I held on to people God was trying to pull away from me.

But the more life tested me, the more I learned this truth:

A woman who knows her worth doesn't fear losing someone; she fears losing herself while trying to keep someone.

And I had lost myself too many times.

This chapter isn't about blaming anyone.
It's about acknowledging the moment I realized *I* had the power to change my story.

Every grown woman reaches a point where she understands she doesn't have to accept the love that breaks her, the friendships that drain her, or the family patterns that repeat themselves generation after generation.

Every woman eventually chooses:

Do I stay who I was taught to be, or do I become who I truly am?

I chose myself.

And choosing myself didn't mean I became selfish, it meant I finally became honest.

- Honest about my needs.

- Honest about my boundaries.

- Honest about my expectations.

- Honest about what hurts me.

- Honest about what I deserve.

- Honest about who deserves a place in my life.

Choosing myself meant walking away from men who didn't respect me.

• It meant letting go of friendships that were one-sided.

• It meant distancing myself from family members who only showed up for drama.
It meant outgrowing people who were comfortable with my brokenness but intimidated by my healing.

• It meant learning that I don't have to tolerate disrespect from anyone — not a man, not a woman, not family, not a friend.

• It meant learning that God never meant for me to shrink myself just to fit inside someone else's comfort zone.

• It meant learning that my voice matters, my happiness matters, my peace matters, my boundaries matter, and my love is valuable.

If you are reading this, I want you to know something:

You are not reading the words of a perfect woman.

You are reading the words of a woman who survived herself.

There is a difference.

Surviving other people is one thing.

Surviving the old version of yourself is another battle entirely.

- I had to survive the version of me who always said yes.

- Who always forgave.

- Who always explained herself.

- Who always stayed too long.

- Who always believed the lies.

- Who always hoped people would change.

- Who always put everyone else first.

And when that old version of me finally died, people got uncomfortable.

- They weren't used to my "no."

- They weren't used to my silence.

- They weren't used to my boundaries.

- They weren't used to my peace.

- They weren't used to me walking away without announcing it.

But I had reached a point where losing myself was no longer an option.

That is why this book exists.

- Because women need to hear these truths.

- Because too many of us survive but don't grow.

- Because too many of us heal but don't change.

- Because too many of us leave situations but keep the same mindset.

- Because too many of us are "strong" but secretly tired.

- Because too many of us keep quiet to keep the peace.

- Because too many of us don't know we deserve more.

This book is not about heartbreak; it is about what heartbreak taught me. It is not about pain, it is about power. It is not about the past; it is about the woman I refuse to stop becoming. And if you take anything from this chapter, let it be this:

- You are allowed to rewrite who you are at any age.

- You are allowed to choose yourself without guilt.

- You are allowed to outgrow people who stop growing.

- You are allowed to expect respect.

- You are allowed to want love that doesn't hurt.

- You are allowed to be unbroken, again and again.

The woman I became after the hurt is not perfect, but she is honest. She carries more wisdom now, more strength, more softness where her heart calls for it and more toughness where life requires it. She walks closer to God, protects her peace fiercely, and stays loyal to herself before anyone else. She remains hopeful, never desperate; loving, but no longer blind. She is no longer afraid to walk alone, to walk away, or to speak the truth that lives in her spirit: "I deserve more." This is her story. This is my story. And now it becomes yours too, because every woman reaches a moment when she finally becomes herself. And when she does, she becomes unbreakable.

Still unbroken.

CHAPTER TWO:

WHEN RESPECT MEANS MORE THAN LOVE

Love is a powerful word. People say it easily. People promise it freely. But love, by itself, has never been enough to keep a woman safe, whole, or honored.

You can love someone who treats you wrong.
You can love someone who lies to you.
You can love someone who embarrasses you, ignores you, or slowly chips away at your spirit.

That is one of the hardest truths to accept. Love does not automatically come with care. Love does not guarantee protection. And love does not always show up as respect.

I learned that early. I watched men say "I love you" while doing things that screamed the opposite. I watched women stay because the word love sounded better than the reality they were living. I watched myself make excuses for behavior that never should have been excused.

Real love does not humiliate you.
Real love does not confuse you.
Real love does not make you feel small in private while pretending in public.

Respect is the first sign of real love. Not gifts. Not sweet talk. Not apologies after damage is done. Respect shows up in how a man speaks to you when he is angry. Respect shows up in how he listens when you are tired. Respect shows up in consistency, not convenience.

A man can claim love all day long. But if he disrespects your time, your body, your feelings, or your boundaries, then love is not what he is offering. Control, comfort, habit, or ego maybe. But not love.

I have seen too many men hide behind that word. They say they love you while cheating. They say they love you while lying. They say they love you while making you feel like you are asking for too much just for wanting honesty and effort.

And one thing I will always stand on is this: how a man treats his mother tells you everything you need to know.

Listen to how he talks about her.
Watch how he speaks to her when no one is watching.
Pay attention to whether he honors her or resents her.

A man who disrespects his mother will eventually disrespect you. It may not happen right away. It may come wrapped in charm at first. But it will show itself. Because if he cannot respect the woman who gave him life, it will be hard for him to truly respect any woman long term.

A man who treats his mother like a queen understands honor. A man who protects his mother understands responsibility. A man who speaks gently to his mother understands restraint. Those things matter more than words ever will.

I still believe in old school love. The kind of love where a man opens doors without being asked. The kind of love where he checks on you because he wants to, not because you reminded him. The kind of love where loyalty is normal, not rare. The kind of love where respect is automatic, not negotiated.

That is the love I pray for. Not perfection. Not fairy tales. Just consistency, honesty, and respect.

Real love does not make you beg to be valued.
Real love does not require you to lower your standards to keep someone comfortable.
Real love does not ask you to accept disrespect in exchange for affection.

Love without respect will drain you.
Love with respect will protect you.

And once you know the difference, you will never accept less again.

CHAPTER THREE:

THE LIES MEN TELL AND THE TRUTH WOMEN IGNORE

Some men do not come to you empty handed. They come with dreams. Beautiful ones. Carefully spoken ones. Dreams about the future, about growth, about forever. They talk about what they want to build, who they want to be, and where they see you fitting into that picture.

That is what I call selling dreams.

They know exactly what to say. They know the right timing. They know how to sound sincere. And too often, women listen with their hearts instead of their eyes.

I have heard the same old lines more times than I can count.

"I'm not like other men."
"I've been hurt before."
"I want something real."
"I just need time."
"I see a future with you."

Those words sound good. They feel good. But words without action are nothing more than noise.

The truth is, many men repeat the same lines because they work. They know women want love. They know women want stability. They know women want to believe. And so they sell hope, even when they have no intention of delivering.

And women, myself included at one time, want to believe even when we should not.

We ignore the gaps.
We excuse the silence.
We explain away the inconsistency.

We tell ourselves he is busy. We tell ourselves he is figuring things out. We tell ourselves things will change once he is ready. What we do not want to admit is that he already knows.

A man knows early what he wants. He does not need years to decide if you are worth committing to. Within six months, a man knows if he wants to move forward or keep his options open. If he is still unsure, still vague, still avoiding clear direction, that uncertainty is your answer.

Men do not stay confused about women they truly want. They may move slowly, but they move with intention. When there is no intention, there is usually another reason. Comfort. Convenience. Access. Control.

That is why I refuse part time love.

Part time love is attention when it suits him.
Part time love is affection without accountability.
Part time love is promises with no follow through.

I have lived that life. I have been the woman who waited for calls that came late. The woman who adjusted expectations to avoid arguments. The woman who accepted crumbs because I hoped they would eventually turn into a meal.

My experiences taught me that red flags do not appear all at once. They show up quietly.

He talks big but moves small.
He avoids defining the relationship.
He disappears and returns like nothing happened.
He gets defensive when you ask honest questions.
He gives you just enough to keep you hoping.

Those signs are not confusion. They are clarity.

Women ignore red flags because hope can be blinding. Because we want the story to end differently. Because we believe our love can change the outcome. But love does not fix dishonesty. Patience does not turn inconsistency into commitment. And silence is never a sign of seriousness.

I learned that the hard way.

Now I watch behavior, not words. I listen to effort, not excuses. I pay attention to how a man shows up when there is nothing in it for him.

The truth women need to hear is simple. If he wanted to, he would. If he meant it, he would show it. If he was serious, you would not be guessing.

Seeing red flags early is not about becoming cold or bitter. It is about becoming aware. It is about protecting your heart before it gets bruised. It is about knowing your worth before someone convinces you to settle for less.

Dreams are beautiful. But only when they are real.

CHAPTER FOUR:

WHEN FAMILY LOVES YOU AND HURTS YOU TOO

Family is supposed to be safe. It is supposed to be where you land when the world gets heavy. But the truth is, family can love you and hurt you at the same time. And learning how to hold both of those truths is one of the hardest lessons of all.

My loyalty to my siblings has always been deep. No matter how mad we got at each other, no matter how far apart life pulled us, I never stopped loving them. We did not always see eye to eye, but we were always connected. That bond did not break just because we argued or disagreed.

When it came to my brother, I was especially protective. There were times I had to stand up for him, times I had to confront people who thought they could speak on him without knowing our story. I do not play about my family. If you do not know us, you do not get to judge us. Respect matters, even when things are not perfect.

I learned early that protecting family does not mean letting them cross every line. You can love your people and still set boundaries. You can defend them in public and still hold them accountable in private. Loyalty does not mean silence when something is wrong, and love does not mean tolerating disrespect.

One of the hardest things to deal with is when siblings disappear. Life gets busy, phones go unanswered, and suddenly you are left handling things on your own. Then, days later, they reappear asking questions, wanting updates, wanting explanations. And all you can think is, Where were you when I needed you?

That kind of distance hurts. Not because you stop loving them, but because you expected more. Sometimes the only answer you have left is never mind. Not out of spite, but out of exhaustion.

Family drama has a way of traveling fast. Stories get twisted. Words get added. Truth gets bent. Gossip finds its way into places it never belonged. I have watched people take pieces of my life and turn them into something unrecognizable, all because they were bored, nosey, or looking for something to talk about.

I learned to be careful with my truth. Not everyone deserves access to your story, even if they share your last name. Some people cannot hold water. By the time a story comes back to you, it is no longer yours. And that is when you realize that boundaries are not about pushing people away, they are about protecting your peace.

Still, love does not disappear. It just becomes layered. Love mixed with frustration. Care mixed with disappointment. Connection mixed with distance.

That is what family often looks like.

You get mad. You argue. You take space. But when someone from the outside tries to cross a line, you show up. You defend. You correct. You remind people that blood still means something, even when it is complicated.

Family is not perfect. It never has been. But it is still sacred. It is history, shared memories, and roots that run deeper than words. Learning how to love your family without losing yourself is not easy, but it is necessary.

Because family will test you.
Family will hurt you.
Family will love you anyway.

And somehow, you learn how to hold all of that at once.

CHAPTER FIVE:

MIND YOUR BUSINESS: THE POWER OF BOUNDARIES

There is one thing about me that has never changed, no matter how old I get or how much life teaches me. I do not like nosy people. I never have. I never will. And the older I get, the less patience I have for people who feel entitled to information that does not belong to them.

I have always believed that curiosity without permission is disrespect. People disguise it as concern, as friendliness, as just wanting to check on you. But most of the time, it is none of that. It is boredom. It is insecurity. It is people wanting something to talk about that has nothing to do with their own lives.

I learned early that not everyone who asks questions actually cares about the answers.

Some people ask so they can judge.
Some people ask so they can repeat.
Some people ask so they can feel important.

And some people ask simply because they cannot stand not knowing something that is not theirs to know.

That is where rumors are born.

Rumors do not start with truth. They start with loose mouths and wandering minds. One person hears something small. Another person hears it halfway.

Another person adds their own assumptions. Before you know it, a whole story exists that you never told and never lived.

I have watched my own life get retold in ways that made me laugh and shake my head at the same time. People would swear they knew what was going on with me, what I was doing, who I was talking to, what I was planning. And I would be sitting there thinking, when did my life become public property?

That is when I realized something important. People will talk whether you give them something or not. Silence does not stop gossip. Privacy does not stop lies. If someone wants to run their mouth, they will find something to say.

So instead of stressing myself out trying to control what people think or say, I changed how I moved.

I stopped explaining.
I stopped over sharing.
I stopped answering questions I did not feel like answering.

And sometimes, when I knew someone was being nosy on purpose, I decided to have a little fun with it.

I would give them a fake story.

Nothing harmful. Nothing serious. Just enough to see what would happen. And every single time, it proved my point. That fake story would grow legs and run. It would get passed around, twisted, stretched, exaggerated. By the time it came back to me, it was unrecognizable.

And instead of being mad, I would laugh.

Because now I knew exactly who could not be trusted. Now I knew who could not hold water. Now I knew who was listening with their mouth instead of their heart.

People think boundaries are about pushing others away. They are not. Boundaries are about protecting yourself from unnecessary stress, drama, and foolishness. Boundaries are about deciding who gets access to you and who does not.

I had to learn that family does not get unlimited access just because they are family. Friends do not get unlimited access just because you have history. And acquaintances definitely do not get access just because they are curious.

Not everyone deserves your truth.

Some people will twist it.
Some people will weaponize it.
Some people will repeat it without context.

And then look at you crazy when you pull back.

One thing about me, when I say stay out of my business, I mean it. And I do not apologize for it. I do not soften it. I do not dress it up in polite language to make someone else feel better.

Stay out of my business means exactly that.

It means do not ask questions you are not prepared to respect the answers to.

It means do not repeat things I trusted you with.
It means do not speak on my life like you live it.

I do not ask people about their finances. I do not ask about their relationships. I do not ask about their family drama. If someone wants me to know something, they will tell me. That is called respect.

And I expect the same in return.

Some people get offended when you set boundaries. That reaction alone tells you everything you need to know. They were benefiting from your lack of boundaries. They were comfortable crossing lines. They were used to having access they never earned.

When you take that away, they call you distant. They call you changed. They call you funny acting.

Let them.

I am not here to be easily accessible to everyone. I am here to live in peace. I am here to protect my mind, my heart, and my energy. I am here to move how I move, without explaining myself to people who do not pay my bills, carry my burdens, or live my life.

I learned that being private does not mean being fake. It means being selective. It means understanding that your life is not entertainment. Your pain is not a topic. Your growth is not a discussion.

I am the same person from beginning to end. How you meet me is how you leave me. I do not change to fit into other people's comfort zones. I do not rewrite myself so others feel important. And I do not lose sleep over what people think when they do not know the full story.

The funny thing is, once I started minding my business and telling others to do the same, my life got lighter. Less drama. Less stress. Less explaining. My circle got smaller, but my peace got bigger.

And I realized something else. People who truly care about you do not need to know everything. They respect your silence. They respect your space. They respect your boundaries without taking it personal.

Everyone else was just noise.

So yes, mind your business is a boundary.
It is a warning.
It is self preservation.

And I stand on it proudly.

CHAPTER SIX:

I DON'T CHANGE FOR NOBODY

People love to say you changed when you stop letting them play with you.

That is one of the first things I learned. The moment you grow, set boundaries, or start standing firm in who you are, somebody will look at you sideways and say, "You're not the same anymore." And they say it like it is an insult. Like changing is a crime. Like evolving means something is wrong with you.

But the truth is, I did not change. I just stopped shrinking.

I am still the same person I have always been. Same heart. Same mouth. Same honesty. Same loyalty. What changed is my tolerance. What changed is my patience for foolishness. What changed is my willingness to explain myself to people who never really listened anyway.

People mistake growth for attitude. They mistake boundaries for coldness. They mistake self respect for being difficult.

And I let them.

I got tired of trying to prove who I was to people who were committed to misunderstanding me. I got tired of softening my words so other people would not feel uncomfortable. I got tired of pretending I did not see what I saw or feel what I felt just to keep the peace.

Peace that costs you your authenticity is not peace at all.

I have always been straightforward. I say what I mean, and I mean what I say. If I love you, you know it. If I do not like something, you will know that too. I do not do fake smiles. I do not do pretending. I do not do being one way in your face and another way behind your back.

Some people cannot handle that.

They want you quiet.
They want you agreeable.
They want you easy to control.

And when you are not, they label you.

"She's changed."
"She's different now."
"She thinks she's better."

No. I just know myself now.

Outgrowing people is a lonely process. Nobody tells you that part. You start realizing that some people only loved the version of you that was convenient for them. The version that did not speak up. The version that accepted less. The version that bent instead of stood tall.

When you stop being that person, they do not know what to do with you anymore.

And that is okay.

I had to learn that not everyone is meant to go where you are going. Some people are seasonal. Some people are lessons. Some people were never meant to grow with you, only around you.

I used to feel bad about that. I used to question myself. I used to wonder if I was being too hard, too blunt, too much.

Then I realized something important. The right people never ask you to dim yourself. The right people do not require you to hide. The right people do not feel threatened by your truth.

So I stopped pretending.

I stopped acting confused when I was not. I stopped saying it was okay when it was not. I stopped laughing at things that hurt me.

I stopped hiding my growth to make other people comfortable.

And let me say this clearly. Loving yourself means staying authentic even when it costs you relationships. Even when it costs you friendships. Even when it costs you access to people who benefited from you being silent.

I love myself enough now to stay true to who I am.

I am not changing my tone to sound nicer. I am not hiding my strength to make someone feel bigger.
I am not shrinking my truth so others can digest it easier.

If who I am makes you uncomfortable, that is not my burden to carry.

I have been through too much to pretend. I have survived too much to lie about who I am. I earned this version of me through pain, loss, lessons, and growth. And I am not apologizing for it.

Some people want you stuck where they met you. They do not want to adjust to your growth. They want access without respect. They want familiarity without accountability.

That will never be me.

I will always be honest. I will always be real. I will always be myself, whether that makes people stay or walk away.

Because at the end of the day, I do not change for nobody. I change for growth. I change for peace. I change for me.

And the ones meant to be in my life will meet me right where I am.

CHAPTER SEVEN:
LESSONS FROM LOVING THE WRONG MEN

Loving the wrong men taught me lessons I never asked for but desperately needed. At the time, I did not see them as lessons. I saw them as love, hope, patience, and effort. I told myself that if I just loved harder, stayed longer, or tried differently, things would change. What I did not understand then was that love can blind you faster than anything else.

Love blinded me to red flags I should have paid attention to. I saw potential instead of patterns. I heard promises instead of truth. I believed words instead of watching behavior. When someone tells you what you want to hear, it is easy to ignore what they are showing you.

I wanted love so badly that I talked myself out of my own instincts. I ignored the tight feeling in my chest when something felt off. I ignored the late nights, the disappearing acts, the half explanations. I ignored the disrespect because I was focused on the good moments, the apologies, the make up conversations that made me feel chosen again.

That is how love blinds you. It makes you focus on what could be instead of what is.

There were moments when I allowed too much. I tolerated things I would never tolerate now. I stayed quiet when I should have spoken up. I accepted excuses that did not make sense. I waited for change that never came. I told myself that relationships required sacrifice, without realizing that I was the only one sacrificing.

I allowed disrespect to creep in slowly. It never started loud. It never showed up all at once. It came disguised as jokes, as misunderstandings, as bad days. It came with apologies that sounded sincere but were never followed by real change. And every time I forgave, I taught them what I was willing to accept.

That part is hard to admit. But it is true.

I did not lose love all at once. Love died piece by piece. Every time I felt dismissed. Every time I felt unheard. Every time I felt like I had to beg for basic respect. Disrespect does not just hurt love. It kills it. Slowly. Quietly. Until one day, you look at the person you thought you loved and feel nothing but exhaustion.

Walking away did not happen overnight either. People think leaving is easy once you know you deserve better. It is not. Walking away means letting go of dreams you held onto for too long. It means accepting that the person you loved is not the person you hoped they would become. It means choosing yourself when your heart still wants to stay.

But there comes a moment when enough is enough.

For me, that moment came when I realized I was losing myself. I was shrinking to fit into spaces I should have never had to squeeze into. I was explaining myself to people who did not care to understand me. I was loving men who were comfortable hurting me.

So I walked away. And when I walked away, I walked away for good.

I did not announce it. I did not argue. I did not beg to be seen or heard one last time. I simply stopped. I chose silence over chaos. Distance over disrespect. Peace over pain.

And that choice changed my life.

Being single now is not loneliness for me. It is protection. It is peace. It is clarity. I no longer wake up anxious about someone else's mood. I no longer question my worth based on someone else's effort. I no longer compromise my standards just to say I am not alone.

I prefer being single because I know what it costs me not to be.

The peace I found after leaving toxic relationships is something I will never trade again. My mind is calmer. My heart is lighter. My spirit is no longer at war with itself. I have space to breathe, to think, to grow, to love myself without interference.

I learned that love should not feel like survival. It should not feel like confusion. It should not feel like constantly proving your value.

Real love starts with self respect.

And once you learn that, you stop loving the wrong men not because you are bitter, but because you are healed enough to choose better.

CHAPTER EIGHT:

FINDING THE SUPPORT YOU DESERVE

One of the biggest lessons I had to learn in life was the difference between people who truly support you and people who only pretend to. At first, they can look the same. They say the right things. They show up when it is easy. They clap when things are going well. But when life gets heavy, when you are tired, confused, or trying to find your footing, the difference becomes clear.

Real support does not disappear when you need it most.

I used to think that anyone who said "I got you" actually meant it. I believed that people who called themselves friends, family, or supporters would naturally stand with me when things got hard. That belief cost me disappointment after disappointment. Because words are easy. Presence is not.

Pretend supporters love to talk.
They love to ask questions.
They love to know what is going on.

But when it is time to listen, they rush you. When it is time to encourage, they minimize your feelings.
When it is time to stand beside you, they step back and watch.

Supportive people are different.

They listen without interrupting.
They do not rush you to be okay.
They do not turn your pain into gossip.

They let you vent. They let you breathe. They let you feel what you feel without making it about themselves.

I learned the importance of having at least one person who truly listens. Not someone waiting for their turn to talk. Not someone already forming opinions while you are still speaking. But someone who hears you fully, without judgment, without dismissal.

Listening is a form of love.

When someone listens to you, they are saying your feelings matter. Your experiences matter. Your voice matters. That kind of support can change the direction of your life.

Encouragement matters more than people realize. Not the fake encouragement that sounds like "it will be okay" with no substance behind it. But real encouragement. The kind that reminds you of who you are when you forget. The kind that pushes you forward without pushing you too hard. The kind that says, "I believe in you," and means it.

I have learned that there is a big difference between people who step in your corner and people who step out when things get uncomfortable.

People who step in your corner defend you when you are not around. They check on you without being asked. They support your growth even when it changes the dynamic. They want to see you win, even if your success does not benefit them.

People who step out do the opposite. They disappear when you need them. They resurface only when it is convenient. They question your decisions instead of trusting your judgment. They show up late and leave early, emotionally and physically.

I have had conversations that changed my direction in life. Simple talks that happened at the right time. Conversations where someone listened to me vent, listened to my frustration, listened to my fears, and then gently helped me see things differently.

Those conversations did not judge me. They did not rush me. They did not tell me what I should do. They asked questions that made me think. They reminded me of my strength. They encouraged me to focus on my purpose, my growth, my future.

Those moments mattered.

They helped me see that not everyone deserves a permanent place in my life. Some people are only meant to be there for a season. Some people are there to teach you what support is not, so you can recognize what it is.

Keeping the right people in your life means being honest about who shows up consistently and who only shows up when it benefits them. It means choosing quality over quantity. It means letting go of people who drain you, confuse you, or make you feel small.

I learned to protect the people who support me. I learned to appreciate the ones who listen, who encourage, who stand firm when things get messy. Those are the people who matter. Those are the people who deserve access to my life.

Real support is not loud. It is steady.
Real support is not dramatic. It is consistent.
Real support does not compete with you. It stands beside you.

Once you recognize real support, you stop settling for anything less. You stop explaining yourself to people who do not listen. You stop expecting depth from shallow connections. And you start building a life surrounded by people who genuinely want to see you whole.

That is when everything begins to change.

CHAPTER NINE:

THE WOMAN WHO CHOOSES HERSELF FIRST

There comes a moment in a woman's life when she realizes that loving everyone else more than herself has cost her too much. It does not happen all at once. It happens slowly, through exhaustion, disappointment, heartbreak, and the quiet realization that she has been showing up for everyone while abandoning herself.

That moment changed me.

Learning to love myself was not easy. It was uncomfortable. It forced me to look at things I had ignored for years. It required me to admit that I had accepted less than I deserved, not because I was weak, but because I did not yet know my worth.

Trauma has a way of confusing love with survival. When you have been hurt, neglected, or mistreated, you start believing that love means enduring pain. You start thinking that being chosen means tolerating disrespect. You convince yourself that if you can just hold on a little longer, things will get better.

But love is not supposed to hurt like that.

I had to rebuild my self worth after trauma. Piece by piece. I had to unlearn the lies I told myself about what I deserved. I had to stop blaming myself for the way others treated me. Abuse is never a reflection of your value. It is a reflection of someone else's brokenness.

I began to understand something powerful. God did not create me to be abused, mistreated, silenced, or broken down. He did not put me on this earth to be someone's punching bag, emotional outlet, or convenience. I was created with purpose, dignity, and value.

That truth changed how I moved.

Setting standards became non negotiable. Standards are not walls meant to keep people out. They are boundaries meant to protect what is sacred. I stopped feeling bad for expecting respect. I stopped apologizing for wanting honesty. I stopped lowering myself to keep others comfortable.

If you cannot meet me with respect, you do not get access to me.

Saying no used to fill me with guilt. I worried about hurting feelings. I worried about being misunderstood. I worried about being seen as selfish. But what I learned is this. Saying no to others is often saying yes to yourself.

No is a complete sentence.
No does not require an explanation.
No does not make you cruel or unkind.

It makes you honest.

Choosing peace over people was one of the hardest but most freeing decisions I ever made. Some people bring chaos disguised as connection. Some relationships drain you more than they fulfill you. Some environments keep you stuck in survival mode.

I had to walk away from spaces that disturbed my spirit. Not because I hated anyone, but because I loved myself enough to stop allowing harm.

Peace is priceless. Once you experience life without constant stress, arguments, or emotional confusion, you realize how heavy things were before. Peace allows you to hear yourself think. It allows you to breathe. It allows you to heal.

Choosing myself did not make me cold. It made me whole.

I learned to speak kindly to myself. I learned to forgive myself for what I did not know back then. I learned to look in the mirror and see a woman who survived, not a woman who failed. I learned to appreciate my strength instead of questioning it.

Self love is not loud. It is quiet and steady. It shows up in the choices you make every day. It shows up in the relationships you allow. It shows up in the way you protect your heart.

I no longer chase validation. I no longer beg to be treated right. I no longer confuse attention with affection. I know who I am now.

I am a woman who chooses herself first.
I am a woman who honors her worth.
I am a woman who knows she was created for more.

And once a woman reaches that place, there is no going back. She becomes unbreakable, not because she is hard, but because she is rooted in love for herself.

CHAPTER TEN:

THE LEGACY I WANT TO LEAVE BEHIND

When I think about legacy, I do not think about money, houses, or things that can be lost or taken away. I think about truth. I think about memory. I think about what will remain of me when my voice is no longer in the room and my hands are no longer here to do the work.

That is why I write.

I am writing my truth so my children and my grandchildren will understand who I really was. Not the version people talked about. Not the version rumors created. Not the version reduced to mistakes or struggles. But the whole woman. The woman who loved hard, fought through pain, stood back up when life knocked her down, and kept going even when she was tired.

I want them to know my strength.

Not the kind of strength that never breaks, but the kind that bends and still survives. I want them to know how much I carried. How much I endured quietly. How many times I chose to keep moving when stopping would have been easier. I want them to understand that strength is not perfection. It is persistence.

There were days I was scared.
There were days I was lonely.
There were days I doubted myself.

But I did not quit. And that matters.

I want my children to read these pages and see that their mother was human. That she made mistakes. That she loved deeply. That she learned lessons the hard way. I want my grandchildren to know that the woman they called Big Mom or Grandma was more than just the person who cooked, laughed, or spoiled them.

I want them to know my story.

I want them to know where I came from so they understand where they come from. I want them to know that pain does not define you, but it can shape you. I want them to know that you can come from broken places and still build something beautiful.

I want to leave them more than memories. I want to leave them wisdom.

The kind of wisdom that says love yourself first.
The kind that says do not accept abuse in the name of love.
The kind that says boundaries are not selfish.

I want them to hear my voice in these words long after I am gone. I want them to feel my presence when they read my stories, laugh at my humor, or pause at my hard truths.

I also want to leave behind the small things that matter more than people realize.

Recipes written down the right way.
Stories told just how they happened.
Lessons passed on without sugarcoating.

Food has always been love for me. Cooking, baking, sharing meals, those were the moments where conversation flowed and hearts softened. I want my grandchildren to cook something I once made and feel close to me. I want them to say, "This tastes like her," and smile.

Legacy is not about being perfect. It is about being real.

It matters because time moves fast. One day you are here, doing everything, holding everything together. And the next day, you are a memory. I want that memory to be honest. I want to be remembered for who I truly was, not who people assumed I was.

I want to be remembered as a woman who loved her family fiercely. A woman who protected her peace. A woman who stood her ground. A woman who chose growth over bitterness. A woman who learned, healed, and evolved.

I want my children and grandchildren to know that everything I did, I did with love. Even when I was strict. Even when I was tired. Even when I said no. I want them to understand that every boundary came from wanting better for them.

Legacy is the quiet way you live your life when no one is watching. It is the values you pass on without realizing it. It is the example you set just by being yourself.

If this book does nothing else, I hope it tells my family this one thing clearly. I was strong. I was real. I was flawed. And I loved deeply.

That is the legacy I want to leave behind.

CHAPTER ELEVEN:

A MESSAGE TO EVERY WOMAN WHO HAS

BEEN BROKEN

This chapter is for you.
Not the woman you pretend to be in public, but the woman you are when the lights are off and the tears fall quietly. The woman who has been hurt, disappointed, silenced, or made to feel small. The woman who kept going even when her heart was tired.

I am talking to you like a sister. Not above you. Not ahead of you. Right beside you.

If you have been broken, I see you.

If you have survived abuse, in any form, emotional, physical, mental, verbal, I need you to hear this clearly. What happened to you was not your fault. Not one piece of it. Abuse does not happen because you loved too much, stayed too long, or tried too hard. Abuse happens because someone chose to harm instead of heal.

You did not deserve that.

I know how easy it is to blame yourself. I know how often women replay moments in their heads, asking what they could have done differently. But the truth is this. Love should never require you to be hurt to be proven real. God did not create you to be beaten down, controlled, or broken in the name of love.

Some of you settled for less because you were tired. Tired of starting over. Tired of being alone. Tired of hoping. You convinced yourself that something was better than nothing. You told yourself it was not that bad. You minimized your pain because you thought that was what strength looked like.

But settling slowly kills your spirit.

Some of you forgot your worth because life hit you hard. Trauma has a way of making you forget who you are. It convinces you that this is all you deserve. That you should be grateful someone chose you at all. That you should stay quiet and accept what is given.

That is a lie.

Your worth does not decrease because someone failed to see it. Your value was placed on you by God, not by a man, not by a relationship, not by someone else's opinion.

To the women still in toxic relationships, I know leaving is not simple. I know it is scary. I know there are memories, promises, children, finances, fear, and hope tangled together. I know some of you are praying for change while your heart is breaking a little more every day.

Hear me when I say this. God wants better for you.

Not better excuses.
Not better apologies.
Not better moments in between the pain.

He wants peace for you. He wants safety for you. He wants love that does not require survival.

You do not have to stay where you are hurting.

Leaving does not make you weak. Staying does not make you strong. Strength is choosing life. Strength is choosing yourself. Strength is believing that you deserve more, even when you are scared.

I am not telling you it will be easy. Healing is messy. Walking away hurts. Starting over feels lonely at first. But staying where you are being destroyed will cost you far more than leaving ever will.

I had to learn that the hard way.

God does not call women to suffer in silence. He does not ask us to endure abuse to prove loyalty. He does not confuse pain with purpose. Sometimes the miracle is not the relationship changing. Sometimes the miracle is you finding the courage to leave.

You are not damaged goods.
You are not too much.
You are not asking for too much.

You are worthy of love that is gentle. Love that is respectful. Love that is safe.

And if you are not ready yet, that is okay. This message is not here to pressure you. It is here to remind you that you are not alone. That there is life beyond what you are living right now. That one day, you will look back and realize you were braver than you thought.

Take this one step at a time. Protect yourself. Reach out for help. Talk to someone you trust. Pray for clarity, not excuses.

Most of all, remember this. You do not have to stay where you are hurting. Your story is not over. Your life is not defined by what broke you. And your future can be brighter than anything you have known.

From one woman to another, I am rooting for you.

CHAPTER TWELVE:

STILL UNBROKEN

If you trace my life from the beginning to now, you will not find an easy story. You will find a story marked by loss, confusion, rejection, and pain. You will find moments that could have hardened me, moments that could have destroyed me, moments where giving up would have made sense to anyone looking in from the outside.

But here I stand.

Still breathing.
Still standing.
Still unbroken.

I survived a childhood that tried to convince me I was unwanted. I survived being passed around by circumstances I never asked for. I survived learning what love was supposed to look like by first experiencing what it should never be. I survived heartbreak that cut deep, relationships that drained me, and disrespect that tested my spirit.

I survived gossip that tried to define me.
I survived lies told about my name.
I survived being misunderstood, misjudged, and mislabeled.

People talked. People assumed. People watched from a distance and thought they knew my story. But they never knew the nights I cried alone. They never knew the strength it took to keep going when I felt invisible.

They never knew how often I had to choose myself just to survive.

I survived trauma that left marks no one could see. Trauma that taught me how strong I had to become before I ever felt safe. Trauma that tried to convince me that pain was normal and peace was unrealistic.

But I learned.

I learned that survival is not the same as living. I learned that love without respect is not love. I learned that peace is worth protecting at all costs.

And most importantly, I learned that broken does not have to be the end of the story.

I am still unbroken not because life was kind to me, but because I refused to let life take everything from me. I refused to let bitterness replace my heart. I refused to let pain turn me cold. I refused to become the things that hurt me.

That does not mean I am perfect. It means I am resilient.

I still hope. That surprises people sometimes. After everything I have been through, they expect me to shut my heart down completely. But hope is not weakness. Hope is strength. Hope is believing that life can still be good, even after it has been hard.

I still hope for love. Not desperate love. Not confusing love. But honest, respectful, peaceful love. The kind of love that feels safe. The kind that adds to your life instead of draining it.

I still hope for peace. Peace in my mind. Peace in my home. Peace in my spirit. Peace that is not disturbed by chaos, drama, or people who thrive on confusion.

I still hope for a life that feels full. Not full of noise, but full of meaning. Full of laughter. Full of moments that remind me why surviving was worth it.

And if love comes, I welcome it with wisdom now. If it does not, I am still whole.

That is something I fought hard to learn.

My message to the world is simple. You never know what someone has survived just to be standing in front of you. Be careful with people's hearts. Be gentle with stories you did not live. Be respectful of strength you did not have to build.

And to anyone reading this who sees themselves in my words, know this. You are not weak because you were hurt. You are not broken because you struggled. You are not behind because your journey looks different.

You are still here.
You are still breathing.
You are still becoming.

And that means you are still unbroken.

This is not the end of my story. It is the proof that I made it through. And if my life has taught me anything, it is this. As long as you are standing, there is always hope.

ABOUT THE AUTHOR

Tonia A. Strickland is a woman who survived what should have broken her. Born into a childhood marked by abandonment and foster care, she learned early what pain felt like, but she also learned how strength grows in the middle of storms. Raised by the grandmother who became her true mother, Tonia found love in the places where God planted it and built her own life on resilience, hard work, and faith.

As a mother, grandmother, survivor, and truth-teller, Tonia has lived through experiences that shaped her into the woman she is today. She has faced abuse, heartbreak, family struggles, loss, and betrayal, yet she continues to rise, stronger each time, carrying the lessons with her. Her voice is unfiltered, honest, and deeply human, speaking directly to women who have endured the weight of love, the silence of pain, and the fight to find themselves again.

Her first book, *Unbroken,* shared the story of her early life, including the wounds, trauma, and her journey toward healing. Her second book continues that reflection, revealing the wisdom she gained as a grown woman learning to choose herself, value her worth, and expect the respect she deserves.

Tonia writes to help others feel less alone. She opens the door to conversations many are afraid to have, shining a light on genuine relationships, family truths, boundaries, and the importance of self-love. Her storytelling blends strength with vulnerability, reminding readers that no matter what they've been through, they can still stand tall.

When she is not writing, Tonia enjoys baking, spending time with her family, sharing laughter, and focusing on the legacy she wants to leave behind for her children and grandchildren. Every page she writes is a piece of her truth, a reminder that life can bruise you, but it cannot break you unless you let it.

Tonia A. Strickland is, and always will be, **still unbroken**.

9 781968 845209